Mishkan R'fuah

Where Healing Resides

Mishkan R'fuah

Where Healing Resides

EDITOR
Rabbi Eric Weiss

CONSULTING EDITOR
Rabbi Shira Stern, *D.Min., BCC*

Central Conference of American Rabbis
5773 New York 2013

10 9 8 7 6 5 4 3 2 1

LIBRARY OF CONGRESS CATALOGING-IN-PUBLICATION DATA
Mishkan r'fuah : where healing resides / [edited by] Eric Weiss ;
consulting editor, Shira Stern.
    p. cm.
 Includes bibliographical references and index.
 ISBN 978-0-88123-196-0 (pbk. : alk. paper)
1. Benediction—Judaism. 2. Judaism—Liturgy. I. Weiss, Eric, 1956–
II. Stern, Shira.

  BM523.3.B4M57 2012
  296.7′6—dc23
                    2012035180

Cover Art: Michelle's Chuppah © 2012 by Iris Sonnenschein,
www.irisquilts.com. Commissioned by Myra Tattenbaum for her
daughter's wedding. Used with permission.

Interior design and typography by Scott-Martin Kosofsky
at The Philidor Company, Lexington, Massachusetts.

CCAR PRESS
355 Lexington Avenue, New York, NY 10017
(212) 972-3636
www.ccarpress.org

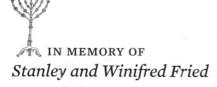 IN MEMORY OF

Stanley and Winifred Fried

Dedicated to the many patients for whom we all care throughout the generations. May this prayer book help us to find strength and healing.

—*Joanne B. Fried*

Advisory Committee

Rabbi Ruth Alpers

Rabbi Pearl Barlev

Rabbi Seth Bernstein, *BCC*

Rabbi John Fishman

Rabbi Jo Hirschmann, *BCC*

Rabbi Debra Kassoff

Rabbi Richard Kellner

Rabbi Elliot Kukla

Rabbi Jon Sommer

Rabbi Julia Weisz

Rabbi Hara E. Person,
  Director and Publisher, CCAR Press

Rabbi Steven A. Fox,
  Chief Executive,
  Central Conference of American Rabbis

Contents

Spiritual needs have a great range. We may need to invoke Awe, seek some clarity of feeling, question God or in some other way nourish a yearning that may often seem wordless. This Table of Contents reflects a range of life circumstances in which are embedded spiritual response. You may find that a prayer outside of your own circumstances articulates something about your own spiritual need nonetheless. We encourage you to engage this Table of Contents for both its listing of specific prayers and to explore where a prayer that might otherwise appear unrelated to you can respond to your spiritual need. We hope that this kind of spiritual empathic stretch will bring us all closer to one another.

Note: Some of the readings end with the word "amen". "Amen" is potent in our tradition in part because it typically underscores a communal affirmation that the words uttered are embedded with a spiritual desire for Divine consideration. "Amen" appears here in both those readings in which the piece itself inherently assumes a group may be present, and where it reflects the author's stylistic consideration. However, "amen" can be an appropriate response to any of the readings should the private reader desire.

Acknowledgments

"Thank you" in Hebrew is *todah*. It shares the same root as the word *hodaah*, "gratitude," found as part of our communal recitation of hopes and dreams in the backbone of our liturgical canon called the *Amidah*. "Thank you" in our tradition recognizes the innate layers of relationship that yield all accomplishment. Just as a miracle drug comes into our hands by the hard work of countless teams of people, this resource is filled with the constellation of many conversations, dedicated souls, and inspired voices. No one succeeds alone. All spiritual care comes into our communal life from many hearts.

The committee's efforts to shape this work is myriad, from Seth Bernstein's suggestion of "Where Healing Resides" to the suggestions, wordsmithing, field testing, and teleconferences of many individuals. To Rabbis Ruth Alpers, Pearl Barlev, Seth Bernstein, John Fishman, Jo Hirschmann, Debra Kassoff, Rick Kellner, Elliot Kukla, Jon Sommer, and Julia Weisz—*todah*. A particular *todah* for Shira Stern's efforts and wisdom. In addition to the committee, thanks to Cantor Susan Caro, Rabbi Eliot Baskin, and Rabbi Nathan Goldberg, who field-tested material in their respective settings. And to all the members of the CCAR Worship and Practice Committee who offered additional suggestions and feedback, Rabbis Elaine Zecher (chair), David Adelson, Nicole Greninger, Rosie Haim, Tamar Malino,

Joel Mosbacher, Rex Perlmeter, Beth Schwartz, Joel Sisen-wine, Joseph Skloot, and Alison Wissot—*todah*. *Todah* also to Rabbis who were especially helpful: Rabbis Melanie Aron and Phyllis Somer.

Our movement is at a transition point. For any kind of Judaism, spiritual response must be planted into its terrain so that it can choose life. For the countless unanticipated moments of rooted growth, thank you to our colleague Rabbi Hara Person.

To everyone at the CCAR who helped make this resource a reality, including Rabbi Steven Fox, Debbie Smilow, Rabbi Jillian Cameron, rabbinic intern Yael Rooks-Rapport, Debra Hirsch Corman, Ortal Bensky, and to our colleague Rabbi Bob Loewy—*todah*.

The interplay between Torah and *kemach* is an ancient one. *Todah* to Joanne Fried, who believed in this book and whose mitzvah has brought it into the hands of so many in need.

With gratitude, *todah* to the board of the Bay Area Jewish Healing Center: Neal Tandowsky, Nancy Boughey, Mary DeMay, Gregg Rubenstein, Lenore Bleadon, Rabbi Michael Barenbaum, Martin Brotman, Elizabeth Hausman, Allan Kaplan, Ginny Lawrence, Rabbi Sheldon Marder, Deborah Lederer Sagues, Samele Samuel, Arlene Singer, and staff members Rabbi Natan Fenner, Gail Kolthoff, Rabbi Elliot Kukla, and Rabbi Jon Sommer for their dedication to the field of Jewish spiritual care. The investment of the wider Bay Area Jewish community has been a vital source of succor that has sustained the often confidential work at the bedside. Every hand is held by every supporter. And finally, a speechless *todah* to my husband, Dan.

A Note on Usage

All healing is a journey toward wholeness. Most of us know ourselves best when we are healthy and well. When we become ill, we are suddenly estranged from our familiar surroundings and often from ourselves. It is as if we are in a foreign terrain with no guide. While the primary framework of this healing book, *Mishkan R'fuah: Where Healing Resides*, is designed to articulate the spiritual experience wherever one engages medical attention, from the hospital bed to the clinician's office to one's home, it also includes some of the human experiences in which spiritual yearning may come to the fore, such as when facing incarceration. We all know that when one person needs medical care, the impact is felt by those around them. We hope this book will be nourishing for loved ones, family, and caregivers as well. The experience in the clinical setting may range from childbirth to a day procedure, from an emergency to a long-term stay. This spiritual resource seeks to meet the needs that reflect both the feelings that arise while in the hospital as well as specific reasons for hospitalization. We hope that the words on these pages will decrease isolation, buoy the spirit, bring clarity to the soul's expression, and invoke communal care.

Preface

Progress is an intricate relationship between the betterment of life and the new challenges it produces. Our human imagination yields discovery throughout the landscape. In science, the arts, theology, and the like, we have brought about a civilization that looks both outward and inward to form a way to live as fully as possible. As we advance our medical capacity, make new technology commonplace, and define the human experience with new vocabulary, so too our capacity for spiritual expression must reflect our deepest yearnings. The trajectory of discovery will always look to bring life into this world more easily, invest in new ways to sustain life, and bring the dreams of cure into reality. Vaccines, antibiotics, surgery, in vitro fertilization—these are just a few examples of progress that has enriched us. So too our evolving spiritual world has provided a backdrop for sustaining us: meditation, the commonplace of mindfulness, seeking a personal relationship to God in the midst of a communal life, weaving ancient texts into the individual worldview—these are just a few examples of soul-sustaining efforts in an evolving civilization.

All progress both fossilizes some human forms of expression and at the same time births new forms; our prayer books have changed translations and attended to issues of gender. All theology strives to frame progress into ritual, prayer, and spiritual reflection. We will never tire of this poetry, because it is the endless form with which we express our deepest yearnings. Spiritual reflection—in prayer or ritual—is the form that allows us to link our history to our personal story. It is a glimpse into a moment of life that longs to be held, to find comfort, to strive toward wholeness. From the religious to the secular, our natural spiritual hunger seeks nourishment. From holiday to holiday and from one individual life event to the next, we write our communal and personal narratives into a life's story.

This healing book, *Mishkan R'fuah: Where Healing Resides*, is an effort to provide the spiritual sustenance we all crave in the midst of life's vulnerabilities, whether at the moments of the first breath or the last, whether at the singular procedure or during the ongoing engagement with medicine. At any moment along a spiritual journey we can be filled with either surety or doubt. We may struggle with language, metaphor, and theology, or we may find them satisfying. Our hope is that the moment you enter into prayerful engagement here, the experience will bequeath you, across the millennia, your place within our people's unbreakable relationship to God, Torah, and Israel. Progress in any endeavor brings the soul's yearnings into new arenas of expression. We hope that this healing book will weave our human capacity for discovery into our capacity for spiritual life.

Part I
Building a Tent of Healing

Illness, coming to the end of life, and living with grief are universal human experiences. No one gets through life unscathed. These universal human experiences naturally stimulate spiritual reflection. They reasonably yearn for a communal response. Everyone needs help. We are knit into a vast community of interrelationship. We depend on many to diagnose, perform a test, feed us, and help us to be comfortable in a place that is so vulnerable that it feels alien. We are interdependent. We need a myriad of voices to help us bring expression to the deepest yearnings we have to be whole.

Traditional *Mi Shebeirach* (male)

מִי שֶׁבֵּרַךְ אֲבוֹתֵנוּ וְאִמּוֹתֵנוּ,
אַבְרָהָם, יִצְחָק וְיַעֲקֹב,
שָׂרָה, רִבְקָה, רָחֵל וְלֵאָה,
הוּא יְבָרֵךְ וִירַפֵּא אֶת־הַחוֹלֶה _____ בֶּן _____.
הַקָּדוֹשׁ בָּרוּךְ הוּא יִמָּלֵא רַחֲמִים עָלָיו
לְהַחֲלִימוֹ וּלְרַפֻּאוֹתוֹ, לְהַחֲזִיקוֹ וּלְהַחֲיוֹתוֹ.
וְיִשְׁלַח לוֹ בִּמְהֵרָה רְפוּאָה שְׁלֵמָה, רְפוּאַת הַנֶּפֶשׁ
וּרְפוּאַת הַגּוּף, בְּתוֹךְ שְׁאָר חוֹלֵי יִשְׂרָאֵל,
הַשְׁתָּא בַּעֲגָלָא וּבִזְמַן קָרִיב, וְנֹאמַר: אָמֵן.

Mi shebeirach avoteinu v'imoteinu,
Avraham, Yitzchak v'Yaakov, Sarah, Rivkah, Rachel v'Lei-ah,
hu y'vareich virapei et hacholeh _____ ben _____.
HaKadosh Baruch Hu yimalei rachamim alav
l'hachalimo ulrapoto, l'hachaziko ulhachyoto.
V'yishlach lo bimheirah r'fuah shleimah, r'fuat hanefesh
urfuat haguf, b'toch sh'ar cholei Yisrael,
hashta baagala uvizman kariv, v'nomar: Amen.

May the One who blessed our ancestors, Abraham, Isaac, and Jacob, Sarah, Rebecca, Rachel, and Leah, bless and heal [*name*]. May the Blessed Holy One be filled with compassion for his health to be restored and his strength to be revived. May God swiftly send him a complete renewal of body and spirit, and let us say, Amen.

Traditional *Mi Shebeirach* (female)

מִי שֶׁבֵּרַךְ אֲבוֹתֵנוּ וְאִמּוֹתֵנוּ,
אַבְרָהָם, יִצְחָק וְיַעֲקֹב,
שָׂרָה, רִבְקָה, רָחֵל וְלֵאָה,
הוּא יְבָרֵךְ וִירַפֵּא אֶת־הַחוֹלָה _____ בַּת _____.
הַקָּדוֹשׁ בָּרוּךְ הוּא יְמַלֵּא רַחֲמִים עָלֶיהָ
לְהַחֲלִימָהּ וּלְרַפְּאוֹתָהּ, לְהַחֲזִיקָהּ וּלְהַחֲיוֹתָהּ.
וְיִשְׁלַח לָהּ בִּמְהֵרָה רְפוּאָה שְׁלֵמָה, רְפוּאַת הַנֶּפֶשׁ
וּרְפוּאַת הַגּוּף, בְּתוֹךְ שְׁאָר חוֹלֵי יִשְׂרָאֵל,
הַשְׁתָּא בַּעֲגָלָא וּבִזְמַן קָרִיב, וְנֹאמַר: אָמֵן.

Mi shebeirach avoteinu v'imoteinu,
Avraham, Yitzchak v'Yaakov, Sarah, Rivkah, Rachel, v'Lei-ah,
hu y'vareich virapei et hacholah _____ bat _____.
HaKadosh Baruch Hu yimalei rachamim aleha
l'hachalimah ulrapotah, l'hachazikah ulhachyotah.
V'yishlach lah bimheirah r'fuah sh'leimah, r'fuat hanefesh
urfuat haguf, b'toch sh'ar cholei Yisrael,
hashta baagala uvizman kariv, v'nomar: Amen.

May the One who blessed our ancestors, Abraham, Isaac,
and Jacob, Sarah, Rebecca, Rachel, and Leah, bless and heal
[*name*]. May the Blessed Holy One be filled with compassion for her health to be restored and her strength to be
revived. May God swiftly send her a complete renewal of
body and spirit, and let us say: Amen.

Debbie Friedman's *Mi Shebeirach*

מִי שֶׁבֵּרַךְ אֲבוֹתֵֽינוּ
מְקוֹר הַבְּרָכָה לְאִמּוֹתֵֽינוּ

Mi shebeirach avoteinu
M'kor hab'rachah l'imoteinu

May the Source of strength who blessed the ones before us
Help us find the courage to make our lives a blessing,
And let us say, Amen.

מִי שֶׁבֵּרַךְ אִמּוֹתֵֽינוּ
מְקוֹר הַבְּרָכָה לַאֲבוֹתֵֽינוּ

Mi shebeirach imoteinu
M'kor hab'rachah la-avoteinu

Bless those in need of healing with *r'fuah sh'leimah,*
The renewal of body, the renewal of spirit,
And let us say, Amen.

Mi Shebeirach

Fountainhead of all life,

You who rained Your blessings on our mothers
Sarah, Rebecca, Leah, and Rachel
And on our fathers
Abraham, Isaac, and Jacob,

Causing their seed to sprout and grow and thrive
Not only in a land flowing,
But in the desert places too;

May You likewise shower us, their offspring,
And those near to us,
With a recovery of wholeness,
A restoration of the vessel and its contents.

May You pour Your healing into the barren furrows
When we are parched by illness and pain,
Dried out by distancing and despair.

As You have given us Your Torah,
The waters of life,
As a source of help for all time,
Send the waters of healing to all
Who thirst for peace, for wholeness, for *shleimut*.

Prayer for Comfort and Healing

God, Holy One of Blessing: I come before You with many feelings. I have accomplished much and yet wanted more. My acts have given love to others. My words have given encouragement and comfort. Yet, there are actions I wish I had taken, words I wish I had spoken. Some I wish I could take back. There are accomplishments I wanted to achieve but did not. I have apologized for hurts I have caused. I have forgiven others. Sometimes my feelings are clear; sometimes they are not. I pray that whatever the stirrings of my heart, they bring me closer to my true self, to my loved ones, and to You. Created by You, I seek to live ever more fully in Your image. I seek peace for myself and my loved ones. At this time may my life be filled with warmth and wholeness, comfort and healing. Amen.

Meditation on Healing

When I panic, God, teach me patience. When I fear, teach me faith. When I doubt myself, teach me confidence. When I despair, teach me hope. When I lose perspective, show me the way—back to love, back to life, back to You.

Prayer for God's Love

We are loved
by an unending love.
We are embraced
by arms that find us
even when
we are hidden from ourselves.
We are touched
by fingers that soothe us
even when
we are too proud for soothing.
We are counseled
by voices that guide us
even when
we are too embittered to hear.

We are loved
by an unending love.
We are supported
By hands that uplift us
even in
the midst of a fall.

We are urged on by eyes that meet us
even when
we are too weak for meeting:

We are loved by an unending love.
Embraced, touched, soothed, and counseled . . .
ours are the arms, the fingers, the voices;
ours are the hands, the eyes, the smiles;
we are loved
by an unending love.

Psalm Eighty-Five

In Iyar: Ani Adonai Rofecha
A Song of Healing

After this long night of weakness,
I wake again in the morning of return;
Shaking off the tenors and the dreams,
I open my lips to the Eternal.

You are my Strength and my Hope,
The Author of my healing
You are my Promise and my Courage,
Guiding the steps I take toward healing.

After the winter's darkness and biting cold,
The hidden-awayness of my illness,
The isolation, the fear that settled upon me,
I rise with renewed strength to praise You.

You are the Wonder of new life,
Warming, healing sun upon my head;
You restore my concern for others,
As I relinquish my constant self-inventory.

You come to me as spring comes,
Circling back to heal the ravaged earth;
You rest Your hand of blessing on my shoulder
And I sigh with relief at Your concern.

I look for You, Divine Physician,
Even as I begin again to take up my life;
I look for You, Complete Healer,
As I begin again.

Prayer for Mercy

Give ear, O Eternal, to my prayer,
heed my plea for mercy.

In my time of trouble I call You,
for You will answer me.

When pain and fatigue are my companions,
Let there be room in my heart for strength.

When days and nights are filled with darkness,
Let the light of courage find its place.

Help me to endure the suffering and dissolve the fear;
Renew within me the calm spirit of trust and peace.

בָּרוּךְ אַתָּה, יְיָ, רוֹפֵא הַחוֹלִים.

Baruch atah, Adonai, rofei hacholim.

We praise You, O God, Healer of the sick.

Needing Help

God, I don't like to be helped. It makes me feel I am a burden and a nuisance. When I vent anger about my affliction, let me do it privately and with frustration only toward my circumstances, and not toward those who help me. When I must ask for assistance, let my words be gentle. Let me remember to say "please" with even my simplest request and "thank you" when even my smallest bidding is granted. Let me do all that I can for myself. But give me the wisdom to know the difference between self-reliance and foolhardiness. Amen.

The Plague of Darkness

Deliver me from the darkness of my soul,
Created by internal enemies, my defeaters;
They shake the foundation of my being.
They battle my innermost self.

Not as day fades to evening, but as thieves they come,
So abruptly they steal the light
That I stand immobile, mute.
Be again my Light, Holy One, as I seek the light.

Strengthen the stars, remove the obscuring clouds,
Unwrap the blindfold from my eyes;
Renew in my spirit fortitude and strength,
Your precious shard of brilliance, my sunrise.

Take My Hand

When all seems dark and the darkness is harsh,

Take my hand.

When I cannot see light even in the brightest day,

Give me your hand.

When I am tired and every breath is heavy,

Take my hand.

When my words do not grasp the depth of yearning in my soul,

Give me your hand.

When my feelings are overwhelming or dulled,

Take my hand.

When I am confused and don't know what to do,

Give me your hand.

So that we may be together,

Take my hand.

Surround Me with Stillness

Surround me with stillness,
Tiny ripples spreading across the pond.
Touched by one finger of Your hand,
Calmed by the warmth of Your palm.

Croon the wordless melody
That fills my being with peace.

Under the spreading tree of Your affection,
I will sit and meditate
On the goodness You have brought.
Counting the happy moments like glistening beads
Strung to adorn my days.

Light the shadowed corners with gentle glow,
To fill my being with peace.
Drape about me the dappled sunlight of Your teachings,
Opening my eyes to the search,
Clearing my heart of small distractions
That I might find the answers within myself.

Psalm One Hundred Ninety-Nine

I awake bewildered.
As the last dream remnants fade,
And dawn expands to define the day.
I seek You.

Pull me up through clouds of ennui
That threaten my ability to sing to You.
Focus my heart to forge ahead;
Push away the stilled silence.

I am as a snared bird.
My wings cannot lift to flutter
Beyond the trap.
Free me from this weakness.

Fortify me with Your care,
For I am in need of strength;
Firm my loosened limbs
So my lips can open to honor You.

When Fears Multiply

When fears multiply
And danger threatens;
When sickness comes,
And death confronts us—

It is God's blessing of *shalom*
That sustains us
And upholds us,

Lightening our burden,
Dispelling our worry,
Restoring our strength,
Renewing our hope—
Reviving us.

Parents' *Mi Shebeirach* for a Child

אֱלֹהֵי אֲבוֹתֵינוּ וְאִמוֹתֵינוּ

Elohei avoteinu v'imoteinu

God of our fathers and our mothers, as You have cared for the Children of Israel, we ask You to care for our beloved child, [*name*], who is in need of healing. Be with him/her in this time of pain and suffering. Treat him/her with compassion, guard him/her safely through danger, and lend him/her a portion of Your strength.

Share Your strength also with us. Be the Rock that we can lean on, so that we can be a source of support and comfort to our child and to each other. Hold us tightly in Your embrace even as we question and doubt, even as we acknowledge our anger and our fear. Shield and shelter our whole family under the wings of Your loving presence, so that every stopping-place in this journey will be a sanctuary of healing.

בָּרוּךְ אַתָּה, יְיָ, רוֹפֵא הַחוֹלִים.

Baruch atah, Adonai, rofei hacholim.

Blessed are You, Adonai, Healer of the sick.

A Child's *Mi Shebeirach*

Hi God,

I have a lot of thoughts right now.
And lots of feelings.
Many people around me are trying to do a lot of things
    to help me.
Can You help me? I want to get better.
I know that You have done some awesome things and so
I hope that You will listen to me in this moment.
Can you help my doctors to figure things out right?
I wonder if You are also there inside me to help me
    find strength.
Please help me to heal so that I can do the things I
    love to do.
It would help if all the medicines and procedures work, too.
Thanks for taking care of my family and friends.
Thanks for listening.

Amen.

A Prayer for Those Who Help

May the One who blessed and led our forebearers give countenance unto those who provide help for the ill and troubled among us. May they be filled with fortitude and courage, endowed with sympathy and compassion, as they give strength to those at their side. May they fight against despair and continue to find within themselves the will to reach out to those in need. And in their love of others, may they feel the blessing of community and the blessing of renewed faith.

A Medical Practitioner's Prayer

God, uniquely created in Your image, I have used my gifts and talents, my training and experience, to bring my skills to support healing. As I begin this procedure/examination, may I fully appreciate that the work of my hands reflects the work of Yours. May my attentiveness reflect the trust placed in me by each patient, my colleagues, and You. May my work reflect the best I have to offer from the depth of my mind and soul. May the blessing of life and love be ever present to my patients and myself. Amen.

Part II
Entering a Tent of Healing

*Most of us know ourselves and others best when we are well.
Most of us do not know ourselves or others well when we
are ill. As we enter into a Tent of Healing, we can be over-
whelmed by the utter lack of self-knowledge. It is as if we
are suddenly in a foreign land with no guide. New language,
a new environment, new relationships all compound into a
vulnerability that can boggle the mind, numb the heart, and
frighten the soul. As we enter the Tent of Healing, it is important to realize that, for many of us, this is a doorway we did
not want to walk through. And yet, here we are. It is important to look around, to explore the space, to grapple with the
words, the feelings, the reflections that arise, so that we may
hold the hand of those around us and be sustained by our
soul's longing for support.*

On Being Unable to Participate in Jewish Life

O Holy One of Blessing, I find myself in a place where it is difficult to participate in the Jewish life I have built. While my soul yearns for tradition, I face limitations. I feel compromised. I know that above all You and our sages have taught that life must not be endangered. Healing of both body and spirit are a supreme Jewish value, and so I must adjust my involvement to follow Your highest call to care for my health. While we are permitted to forgo some observances in the interest of life and health, I still pray that You understand that I do this not out of neglect, but because of circumstance. As I move through this trying period, O God, please know that I honor as best I can the spirit, intent, and sanctity of what is holy to our people.

On Being Distant

Blessed are You, Shaddai our God, in whom we seek relationship. Like Abraham who challenged You when he saw an injustice and Moses who gave voice to his frustration, I too now beseech You. I find myself in a place of alienation, distant from Your presence. Where are You? Are You in this place? O God, I seek answers, I seek healing, and I seek consolation. The sages called You *HaMakom*, The Place. I reach out to You, and invite You to enter my *makom*, my place. O God, move across this distance and join me. Bless this place, I pray, with Your other great and holy names: Redeemer, Merciful One, and Compassionate One. Amen.

On Anxiety

Adonai, You abide though all things change. I am anxious and fearful, and I turn my heart to You, looking to You and leaning on Your strength.

It is written, "Blessed is the one whose strength is in You." Bless me now with faith and courage. Help me to feel that You are with me, steadying and sustaining me with the assurance that I am loved. Be with me and bring me hope, that in the days to come, my aspirations may be fulfilled for my good and the good of those I love who depend on me. Banish my fears with the sense that You are always present, to uphold and sustain me, as it is written, "Have no fear, for I am with you; be not dismayed, for I am your God. I will strengthen you, I will help you, I will uphold you with the power of My righteousness" (Isaiah 41:10). Amen.

New Chances

Modeh ani l'fanecha
I am so grateful to You,
Melech chai v'kayam
The Great One of life and time
Shehechezarta bi nishmati
That You return my soul each morning
Rabbah emunatecha
How great is Your faithfulness to me

Today Has Been So Hard

Source of All Creation,

Today has been so hard. The doctors have called with more bad news. When hope is gone, where can I find comfort? Where can I find You in this dark time?

Help me to find the strength to face what is ahead. Give me the wisdom to live each remaining moment with my loved one(s) to the fullest.

Shelter my whole family beneath your wings of peace. I am grateful for all the wonderful times we have had. May those memories continue to comfort and inspire us.

Amen.

Prayer for Surgery

אֱלֹהֵֽינוּ וֵאלֹהֵי אֲבוֹתֵֽינוּ וְאִמּוֹתֵֽינוּ

Eloheinu v'Eilohei avoteinu v'imoteinu

Our God and God of all the generations of our people, we pray for healing and for health. Guide the surgeon's hand to bring me health and renewed strength. Support my family as they wait through the hours to come. Be with us all as we seek comfort and the strength to comfort one another.

רוֹפֵא כָּל הַחוֹלִים

Rofei kol hacholim

God who heals the sick, may the healing power of Your presence protect all those who face illness and surgery.

As the prophet said,

רְפָאֵֽנִי, יְיָ, וְאֵרָפֵא

R'fa-eini, Adonai, v'eirafei

"Heal me, O God, and I will be healed."

A Prayer for One Approaching Surgery or Crisis

God, You are with me in my moments of strength and of weakness. You know the trembling of my heart as the moments pass.

Grant wisdom and skill to the mind and hands of those whose lives touch mine.

Grant that I may return to fullness of life and wholeness of strength, not for my sake alone but also for those about me. Enable me to complete my days on earth with dignity and purpose. May I awaken to know the depth of Your healing power now and evermore. Amen.

A Child's Surgery

God of health and healing,
I surrender my daughter/son to the physician's hand,
The surgeon's skill,
The nurse's care,
Placing her/his body into the cradle of others,
Just as I pray for You to hold her/his soul with Your
    loving hands.
Bless her/his surgeon with a steady hand,
Keen vision, and a passion for healing.
Bless her/his caregivers with focus and compassion,
With wisdom and dedication.
Bless our family with comfort and kindness,
Energy and endurance, tranquility and strength.

Source of life,
Bring Your healing power to [child's name].
Remove her/his pain,
Relieve her/his distress,
And restore her/his body, mind, and spirit,
Renewing her/him to wholeness and peace.
Bless her/him with vigor, courage, and hope
So that she/he may experience life and health,
Joy and love.
And grant her/him a full and speedy recovery.

Blessed are You, God of mystery,
Source of health and healing.

Asher Yatzar (The One Who Forms)

A prayer of gratitude for our bodies as men, women, intersex,
transgender people, and everybody else

Blessed are You, Eternal One our God, Ruler of the universe,
who has formed the human being with wisdom.

You created in the human body openings upon openings
and cavities upon cavities. It is clear and well-known that
if just one of these unique valves within the complexity of
each body was blocked or ruptured, it would be impossible
to survive. May the day come when it is also obvious and
evident that if just one unique body within the complexity of Your world is blocked or ruptured, if just one of us is
not allowed to make our distinctive beauty manifest in the
world, then it is impossible for all of Your creation to thrive
and rise each day joyfully before You. Blessed are You,
Source of all life and form, who implanted within us the
ability to shape and reshape ourselves—molding, changing,
transitioning, and adorning our bodies—so that the fullness
of our many genders, the abundance of our desires, and the
diversity of our souls can be revealed.

Blessed are You, Eternal One, who has made me Your
partner in daily completing the task of my own formation.

For Beginning Treatment

אֱלֹהֵינוּ וֵאלֹהֵי אֲבוֹתֵינוּ וְאִמּוֹתֵינוּ

Eloheinu v'Eilohei avoteinu v'imoteinu

Our God and God of our ancestors: as I begin my journey of treatment, I ask for Your guidance and protection. Grant me strength to overcome any obstacles that lie ahead, hope to allow me to persevere even in moments of darkness, and wisdom to be finely attuned to the needs of my body and mind. Grant that those providing medical care may be gentle and compassionate, as You, O God, are gentle and compassionate.

בָּרוּךְ אַתָּה, יְיָ, אֲשֶׁר בְּיָדוֹ נֶפֶשׁ כָּל חַי וְרוּחַ כָּל בְּשַׂר אִישׁ.

Baruch atah, Adonai, asher b'yado nefesh kol chai v'ruach kol b'sar ish.

Praised are You, Adonai, whose hands hold the soul of every living creature.

For Ongoing Treatment

God of Eternality, give me patience.
I am a wanderer; the path before me is long and uncertain.
God of Strength, give me the wisdom to understand
that results are not immediate
but that every day is a victory.
Help me to live each day as a gift
You have set before me.
God of Fortitude, give me the courage to endure,
and in my darkest hours,
remind me that we are all created in Your image.

God of Eternality, give me patience.
I have become a wanderer in time and space.
The waiting and the endless travel from place to place
leave me on a path that is long and unsure.
Perhaps this is truly what a leap of faith feels like,
a singular step, one after the other,
with no clear sense of progress,
uncertainty and hope as my companions on this journey.
God of Strength, let time become a source of wisdom.
Teach me to live each day as best as I can endure.
God of Fortitude, give me courage in my darkest hours.

God of Eternality, give me patience.
I have become a wanderer in time and space.
The waiting and the endless travel
leave me on a path that is long and unsure.
Perhaps this is truly what a leap of faith feels like,
a singular step, one after the other, with no clear
    sense of progress.
Uncertainty and hope are my companions on this journey.
God of Strength, let this path become a source of wisdom.
Help me as I live each day as best as I can endure.
God of Fortitude, give me courage in my darkest hours.

Prayer before Chemotherapy

Harachaman, Merciful One, open the gates of
   Your wondrous
    storehouse releasing Your sparkling dew.

Droplets of life, flow gently, mending the hurt in
   this body of mine,
    watering the vines of this broken garden.
Droplets of blessing, come gently, fetching a year
   of goodness,
    filling with peace the reservoir of my soul.
Droplets of dew, heal gently, softening this hard
   place of blessing,
giving praise to the work of our Creator.

Droplets of dew,
   come for a blessing and not a curse,
   come for life and not for death,
   come bringing plenty and not emptiness.

Upon Conclusion of Treatment

אֱלֹהֵינוּ וֵאלֹהֵי אֲבוֹתֵינוּ וְאִמּוֹתֵינוּ

Eloheinu v'Eilohei avoteinu v'imoteinu

Our God and God of our ancestors: as I arrive at the conclusion of my treatment, I pray for Your blessings. Grant
that the treatment may have lasting impact, helping to
restore me to fullness of mind, body, and spirit. In knowing
sh'leimut, the wholeness that comes with healing, may I also
be blessed to know *shalom*, peace.

בָּרוּךְ אַתָּה, יְיָ, עוֹשֶׂה הַשָּׁלוֹם.

Baruch atah, Adonai, oseih hashalom.

Praised are You, Adonai, source of wholeness,
source of peace.

Choosing to End Treatment

בְּיָדוֹ אַפְקִיד רוּחִי.

B'yado afkid ruchi.

Into Your hands, O God, I entrust my soul. I thank You, God, for wise doctors, nurses, and caregivers, who have combined their skill, compassion, and wisdom in an effort to manage my pain and discomfort and bring me to a place of healing. Grateful for their devotion, I now want to take a different path on my journey toward wholeness.

As I cease treatment, I am not certain of what tomorrow holds in store; I face the future with anticipation and trepidation. I pray that, come what may, You will strengthen me with courage and hope.

Creator of all life, my life is in Your control. Be gentle to me, and ease my suffering. Whether my remaining days are many or few, I pray that You will be with me and with those whom I love throughout the challenges that may lie ahead.

בָּרוּךְ אַתָּה, יְיָ, אֵל רַחוּם וְחַנּוּן לְכָל יְרֵאָיו.

Baruch atah, Adonai, El rachum v'chanun l'chol y'rei-av.

Blessed are You, Adonai, faithful and compassionate God to all who revere You.

Hopeless

God,
Please lift me from this infinite depth.

The light of life and love is so far above it seems like a wisp of a dream from long ago.

The sadness spreads around me reaching to every horizon. If I just lie here, eventually the lifeless air will leave me a desiccated husk of bone and skin who somehow still has the capacity for endless tears.

How did I get here, God?

Sometimes I ask for Your merciful help and implore You to fill me with Your healing grace.

But today I can't even seem to do that.

Abortion

To everything there is a time and a season.
Adonai, the author of beginnings and endings,
be with me now as I let go of this potential life.

There is a time for planting, and a time for uprooting
    the planted.
Allow me my doubts
    even as I remain steadfast in my decision.
Strengthen my soul as I make the choice
    that is right for this time and this season.

There is a time for weeping and a time for laughing.
Adonai, help me to remember
    that as sure as morning follows night,
I too will emerge once again into a new day.
Be with me as I move forward into a time of healing;
be my support as I knit myself back into wholeness.
To everything there is a time and a season.

Birkat HaGomeil
(For One Who Has Escaped Peril)

בָּרוּךְ אַתָּה, יְיָ אֱלֹהֵינוּ, מֶלֶךְ הָעוֹלָם,
הַגּוֹמֵל לְחַיָּבִים טוֹבוֹת, שֶׁגְּמָלַנִי כָּל טוֹב.

Baruch atah, Adonai Eloheinu, Melech haolam,
hagomeil l'chayavim tovot, sheg'malani kol tov.

My thanks to You, bountiful One, Adonai our God, Ruler of
the universe, who in Your inscrutable way watches over the
worthy and the wayward, for having graciously done me
abundant kindness by shielding me from great harm.

Response by those present:

מִי [שֶׁגְּמָלֵךְ /שֶׁגְּמָלְךָ] כָּל טוֹב הוּא
[יִגְמָלֵךְ / יִגְמָלְךָ] כָּל טוֹב, סֶלָה.

Mi [sheg'maleich/sheg'malcha] kol tov hu
[yig'maleich/yig'malcha] kol tov selah.

May God who has shielded you from harm be gracious
to you always.

On Coming Out of Dark Places

Creator,
I have been in such dark places
a flashlight was useless
I have felt fear
no words could comfort me
I seemed lost
and yet
through Your compassion and lovingkindness
I am here, now.
Blessed are You
the Guardian of all
who carries me
to a safe place.

Like a Wave Arising

Like a wave arising from the ocean's dance,
so do we arise from the dance of God.
Like a wave returning from the rocky shore,
its form given to chaos,
but its essence restored in the ocean's unity,
so do we return from life's end
recycled in holiness
to dance once more.
Awesome and wondrous is the Dance of God.

On Recovery

For health of body and spirit, I thank You, my God. I was broken and now am whole; weary, but now am rested; anxious, but now am reassured.

Teach me to show my thankfulness to all who helped me in my need, who heartened me when I was afraid, and who visited me when I was lonely. For the strength You created within me, O God, I give thanks to You.

בָּרוּךְ אַתָּה, יְיָ, רוֹפֵא הַחוֹלִים.

Baruch atah, Adonai, rofei hacholim.

Blessed are You, Adonai, who heals the sick.

A Prayer for Transitioning Gender

May the One who blessed our ancestors—Sarah, Rebecca, Rachel, Leah, Zilpah, and Bilhah; Abraham, Isaac, and Jacob—bless me as I enter into this new chapter in my life. The world was not formed by a single act. Each and every day God renews the work of creation. May God grant me the strength to constantly renew my own creation. May I open my heart and mind to continuous growth, unexpected change, and the perpetual unsettling, liberating expansion of being alive; may I have the courage to name and sanctify this moment of change that is shaping my body and soul in the image of the ever-evolving Divine. Blessed are You, El Shaddai, our God, the Renewing One of the world, who has allowed me to reach this time of transformation. And let us say: Amen.

A Prayer during a Difficult Pregnancy

Help me, God. Help me to endure this time of pain and discomfort. Remind me that this unpleasantness will pass. In the end may my labors be rewarded with a precious new life.

Fill me with strength, God, with patience and stamina and faith. Grant me health, God, and grant health to the sweet, sacred life growing within me. Amen.

Celebrating a Healthy Birth

How small you are, our child, and how beautiful! You grasp
our fingers; we hold you close. Let our arms be your loving
cradle; our whispered prayer, your lullaby.

Our hearts overflow with joy, and we give thanks:

בָּרוּךְ אַתָּה, יְיָ אֱלֹהֵינוּ, מֶלֶךְ הָעוֹלָם,
שֶׁעָשָׂה לָנוּ נֵס בַּמָּקוֹם הַזֶּה.

Baruch atah, Adonai Eloheinu, Melech haolam,
she-asah lanu neis bamakom hazeh.

Praise to You, Adonai our God, Sovereign of the universe,
for the wonder we have experienced.

Blessing for a Premature Birth

May the One who blessed our ancestors bless you, little one, who was born in your own time and at your own hour. May you follow in the footsteps of your ancestor Jacob who arrived after Esau and was not expected, and Peretz, the son of Tamar, who burst forth early surprising the midwives. We say *b'shaah tovah,* may it be in a good hour, and the hour when you were born was truly good, as you are a perfect image of God. It is impossible to predict the exact moment when trees will blossom and give fruit; we can only bless its produce. Likewise, we can only bless the ongoing miracle of your gradual unfolding into life and the miracle of each of your precious breaths. You came into the world at your own time and in your own way; may you continue to grow and thrive along your own unique, curving, and surprising pathways. May we, your parent(s) and your loved ones, have the *z'chut,* the privilege, of raising you to a life of Torah (learning and community), *chuppah* (loving relationships), and *maasim tovim* (good acts).

Things That Are Not To Be

In this world of endless possibilities,
Some things are not to be,
A voiceless answer to my prayers,
An echo of the sounds of creation
A tree uprooted then replanted
The sun tracing a path backward
Across the vast hollow horizon.

Some things are not to be,
The baby that grew tenderly within
Gone now, leaving whispers and flutters
A trail of tears, a mountain-top loneliness
Born from wind and salt and clay.

The body remembers with neural connections
Woven together to embrace me, remind me
You were once here
A frail silvery thread connected
You ever so tentatively to me.

It frayed as the twilight unfolded
The world of endless possibilities
Offered one more thing, not to be:
This loss I wanted to refuse,
The silver thread needs mending
Frail yes, but you were once here.

Not in full form, not in full color
Not full of spirit nor body
And yet something of you lingers.
You belong to the twilight,
You dwell in the whispers,
You echo in my holy tears.

On Miscarriage or Stillbirth

may the name for the Source of Creation be magnified
and my pain grow less and less;
may the will of the Holy One work through me
day by day, hour by hour
so that this raw grief wears thin
and though despair has me, may I know that
the beauty of the world remains
even seen through tears
may I find my way to a place of peace
over this lost child
and may this be my promise:
I will not forget you,
little one I never met
and I ask that the One who makes peace in the high places
(as well as the hidden ones inside)
make peace for you;
give you comfort and angelic shelter
this blessing I ask
for myself
and the one whose life was cut so short

A Prayer When One Experiences Infertility

We have been praying for a child, God, but month after month our hopes have turned to disappointment. Bless us with a child, God. Help me, God. Let me conceive. Turn my envy into love, my despair into hope, my anxiety into calm, my tears into joy. Bless my doctors with wisdom and skill. Let the seed of life be planted and let it take root. Make me fertile, God. Be with me, God; watch over me, hear my prayer. Amen.

A Prayer for Accepting Infertility and Exploring Adoption

God, we want more than anything to have a child. We have tried all the techniques our doctors have to offer. We have lived through a roller-coaster ride of hope and excitement, disappointment and sorrow. I am tired, God. My body is tired.

I still believe in the possibility of a miracle, but perhaps a biological child is not the miracle You have in store for us. I am sad that I may never have the privilege of carrying my child, but perhaps there is a child waiting somewhere at this very moment who is destined to be ours.

We are ready now, God, to begin to explore the opportunity of adoption. Give us the courage, God, to embark on this new journey. Renew our hope. Fill us with the determination and the patience we will need to see this through.

Bless us, God, with a child. Hear this prayer, God. Amen.

Accepting Infertility

Adonai, Source of life and Creator of all, help me to accept
the unacceptable.
It is painful to acknowledge that I have reached the end of
a long and difficult road,
one that I hoped would bring forth a child.
I feel alone and abandoned, denied what I long for most.
I need You now as I struggle against the limits of the
possible.
Comfort me in my grief; console me as I mourn a future
that will not be.
Lend me Your strength so that I can bear the crushing
weight
of this anger and disappointment.
Support me as I struggle to find delight in this world.
Reawaken me to the beauty of Your universe
until I am once again able to envision a future of new
possibilities.
And help me move through despair
so that I will be able to declare with a whole heart:
those who sow in tears will reap in joy.

Accepting Infertility: For a Man

God of Mysterious Power:

So many moments I have imagined all the ways I would
   raise my child.
I have looked forward to being a father;
To hear a child's voice call for me:
In love,
In laughter,
In a cry,
And that I would respond:
To lift,
To hug,
To soothe;
These chances are slipping through my hands.

I fear my shoulder will never feel the warmth of a child's
   breath in surrendered trust.

Please hold me now as I move through this awareness
Toward something I cannot yet grasp.
Catch me, please, in my leap of faith.

TRANSPLANT

Before a Transplant

ORGAN RECIPIENT:

Adonai, created in Your image, I recognize that my body and soul are in Your keeping. I am grateful for the miracles You have given us through medical research and skill and through the generosity of others. Thank You for the possibility of the miracle of life and the relief from suffering that this transplant will bring me and my loved ones. Thank You for the skill of the doctors, nurses, and all those whom I do not know who will care for me as I reach for new possibilities in life.

בָּרוּךְ אַתָּה, יְיָ אֱלֹהֵֽינוּ, מֶֽלֶךְ הָעוֹלָם,
שֶׁגְּמָלַֽנִי כָּל טוֹב.

Baruch atah, Adonai Eloheinu, Melech haolam,
sheg'malani kol tov.

Blessed are You, Adonai our God, Ruler of the universe, who delivers me in complete goodness.

DOCTOR OR MEDICAL STAFF:

Adonai, thank You for the trust You have placed in me as my hands perform Your miracle of sustaining life. May the work of my hands reflect Yours. May blessings come to those I serve, and may I remain ever constant to Your trust in me.

שְׁמַע יִשְׂרָאֵל, יְהוָה אֱלֹהֵינוּ, יְהוָה אֶחָד.

Sh'ma Yisrael, Adonai Eloheinu, Adonai Echad.

Hear, O Israel, God is our Sovereign, God is One.

בָּרוּךְ אַתָּה, יְיָ אֱלֹהֵינוּ, מֶלֶךְ הָעוֹלָם,
שֶׁהֶחֱיָנוּ וְקִיְּמָנוּ וְהִגִּיעָנוּ לַזְּמַן הַזֶּה. אָמֵן.

Baruch atah, Adonai Eloheinu, Melech haolam,
shehecheyanu v'kiy'manu v'higianu laz'man hazeh. Amen.

We praise You, Adonai our God, Sovereign of the
universe, whose nurturance of us as we travel through
life has brought us to this particular time and this
particular place. Amen.

After a Transplant

מוֹדֶה\מוֹדָה אֲנִי.

Modeh/modah ani.

I am truly thankful.

What an incredible gift I have been granted. Through God's loving care, the good skills of my medical team, and the generosity of others, I have been allowed to begin a new chapter.

A new spirit has been placed in me. (based on Ezekiel 36:26)

I am grateful for this gift of life that comes at the expense of another. I will honor the sacrifice it represents by tending carefully that which has been implanted within me.

Teach me, O God, to number my days, that I may gain a heart of wisdom. (Psalm 90:12)

May this miracle remind me always that all people are bound together in a common humanity. May this experience enable me to be more compassionate, more sensitive, and more responsive to those around me. And may I remember to be grateful for every new day, making each day count.

בָּרוּךְ אַתָּה, יְיָ, מְחַיֶּה הַכֹּל.

Baruch atah, Adonai, m'chayeih hakol.

Blessed are You, Adonai, who gives life to everything.

Prayer for Going Home

How I yearned for this—
returning home
returning to life unfettered by hospital regimen
returning to me.
Watch over me as I find my pace,
my peace
my power to heal.

Adonai, guard my coming and my going, to life and peace,
evermore.

T'filat HaDerech

May we be blessed as we go on our way.
May we be guided in peace.
May we be blessed with health and joy.
May this be our blessing, Amen.

May we be sheltered by the wings of peace.
May we be kept in safety and in love.
May grace and compassion find their way to every soul.
May this be our blessing, Amen.

Shehecheyanu

בָּרוּךְ אַתָּה, יְיָ אֱלֹהֵינוּ, מֶלֶךְ הָעוֹלָם,
שֶׁהֶחֱיָנוּ וְקִיְּמָנוּ וְהִגִּיעָנוּ לַזְּמַן הַזֶּה. אָמֵן.

Baruch atah, Adonai Eloheinu, Melech haolam,
shehecheyanu v'kiy'manu v'higianu laz'man hazeh. Amen.

We praise You, Adonai our God, Sovereign of the universe,
whose nurturance of us as we travel through life has
brought us to this particular time and this particular place.
Amen.

Prayer for Renewing Connections with God

In the intimacy of connection, I find You;
People-Linker, You coax the renewal of friendships.
Stymied by inertia, I have neglected these ties,
Slipped the knot that binds me to my story.

So much has changed, so little has changed,
Yet the details are rich and welcomed;
Catch me up again in the warmth of sharing,
Recollecting the reasons for past nearness.

I find You in this reestablished community,
My return from self-imposed separation;
Help to continue this quest of restoration,
Precious reminders of Your light.

Entering into Hospice

God of Acceptance,

I am about to surrender. I will move from the land of medical cure into the land of complete comfort. I am grateful for all that the miracle of medicine has offered me. I know I am at the edge of its capacity. And now I step into the place in which everything lives with Your vision. I want to take Hope with me. I know that Hope before this moment was for the miracle of a full and complete recovery. I have prayed for a *r'fuah sh'leimah*, a recovery of the body and soul. Here I am, before You, my soul filled with a different hope. I hope that You will stay with me. I hope that my soul will know peace. I hope that my body will know no pain. I hope that my life will be seen as valuable. In this moment I give myself to You and all those who will ensure my comfort. My journey continues now into a realm I do not know. When the moment arrives, I will give my last breath to You. Please receive me. Please hold all who care for me. Please hear my voice, even as my speech becomes silent.

Upon Entering into Hospice

God of All Being,
The well of cures has run dry.
My physicians have been focused,
My caregivers diligent,
My family tireless
In their efforts to help me battle this disease.
The horizon of my life nears.
There is a single destination.

Ancient One,
God of our mothers,
God of our fathers,
I surrender my days to You,
As I must,
With the hope of a graceful death,
A dignified death
A loving death.
I make this choice for my own sake,
For the sake of my family and friends,
And for the sake of honoring the life You have given me.

Bless those around me with courage and strength,
Just as I ask You, Holy One,
To grant me the wisdom and ability
To show them my steadfast love,
An inheritance for the generations.

Whatever remains,
The journey hasn't ended.
Ease my pain.
Reduce my suffering.
And bless me, God of my heart,
With fullness of spirit
With moments of faith,
With glimpses of awe and wonder.

Hospice Prayer

Avinu shebashamayim, God in the heavens,
We ask You to look upon _____ and bless him/her.
Let _____ feel Your presence at this time of transition.
Send down Your shining light and fill _____ with that
   light to give him/her peace and comfort.
Shelter _____ from pain.
Guide _____ with Your wisdom and eternal love on
   this final journey.
Let _____ know that he/she will live on in the hearts of
   his/her loved ones.
Bless this family too in this time of deep need. Support
   them when they falter from pain.
Hear our prayer God, for You are a loving God.
Amen.

Vidui

(May be read on someone's behalf.)

אֱלֹהַי וֵאלֹהֵי אֲבוֹתַי וְאִמּוֹתַי . . .

Elohai v'Eilohei avotai v'imotai . . .

My God and God of all who have gone before me, Author of
life and death, I turn to You in trust. Although I pray for life
and health, I know that I am mortal. If my life must soon
come to an end, let me die, I pray, at peace.

If only my hands were clean and my heart pure! I confess
that I have committed sins and left much undone, yet I
know also the good that I did or tried to do. May my acts
of goodness give meaning to my life, and may my errors be
forgiven.

Protector of the bereaved and the helpless, watch over my
loved ones. Into Your hand I commit my spirit; redeem it,
O God of mercy and truth.

*(As the end approaches, the following is said
with or for the dying person:)*

יְיָ מֶלֶךְ, יְיָ מָלָךְ, יְיָ יִמְלֹךְ לְעוֹלָם וָעֶד.

Adonai melech, Adonai malach, Adonai yimloch l'olam va-ed.

God reigns; God has reigned; God will reign
forever and ever.

בָּרוּךְ שֵׁם כְּבוֹד מַלְכוּתוֹ לְעוֹלָם וָעֶד.

Baruch shem k'vod malchuto l'olam va-ed.

Blessed is God's glorious majesty forever and ever.

יְיָ הוּא הָאֱלֹהִים.

Adonai hu ha-Elohim.

Adonai is God.

שְׁמַע יִשְׂרָאֵל, יְהוָה אֱלֹהֵינוּ, יהוה אֶחָד!

Sh'ma Yisrael, Adonai Eloheinu, Adonai Echad!

Hear, O Israel, Adonai is our God, Adonai is One!

THOSE WHO ARE PRESENT:

שְׁמַע יִשְׂרָאֵל, יְהוָה אֱלֹהֵינוּ, יהוה אֶחָד!

Sh'ma Yisrael, Adonai Eloheinu, Adonai Echad!

Hear, O Israel, Adonai is our God, Adonai is One!

(After the moment of death:)

יְיָ נָתַן וַיְיָ לָקָח. יְהִי שֵׁם יְיָ מְבֹרָךְ.

Adonai natan v'Adonai lakach. Y'hi shem Adonai m'vorach.

Adonai gave and Adonai has taken away; blessed be the name of Adonai.

בָּרוּךְ דַּיַן הָאֱמֶת.

Baruch Dayan ha-emet.

Blessed be the Judge of truth.

Forgiveness

My God and witness,
My Creator who knows all hearts,
Look down from the highest mountain
And forgive
And give in love
The *chesed* that comes with repair and healing
To the fissures within my soul
And set my foolish ways aright.
Forgive the flaws that persist in my body
And in my soul that—
Though I did not intend them to be—
Are part of me and all humanity.
Spare me and repair the broken tablets
That, broken, keep me from enlightened faith.
And grant great strength to me
To stand before You
O God!

For One Near Death

Adonai, God of our ancestors, all is now in Your hands.
Forgive and release any hurts or wrongdoings done
    consciously or unconsciously.
Lift up all _____'s worries and fears. Wash them away.
Let goodness flow over him/her and surround him/her now.
Help him/her as he/she readies for his/her next passage.
    May his/her worries for us be eased.
Let him/her know You will walk alongside, and be present
    for us, for his/her soul is entwined with ours.
As he/she comes close to You, bathe him/her in Your light.
    Love him/her and carry him/her.
Shelter him/her under Your wings.
Ready a place in Your garden for him/her.
Into Your hand we trust his/her soul.
Gently, lovingly, tend him/her now.

Adonai blesses you and watches over you.
Adonai's Presence shines upon you and sheds grace
    all around you.
Adonai garbs you in light and bestows peace upon you.

שְׁמַע יִשְׂרָאֵל, יְהוָה אֱלֹהֵינוּ, יְהוָה אֶחָד.
יְיָ הוּא הָאֱלֹהִים.

Sh'ma Yisrael, Adonai Eloheinu, Adonai echad.
Adonai hu ha-Elohim.

Hear O Israel, Adonai our God, Adonai is One.
Adonai is God.

May Your angels come to _____'s sides.
On his/her right, Michael, carry our prayers;
on his/her left, Gavriel, protect him/her;
before him/her, Uriel, light his/her way;
behind him/her, Raphael, heal all hurts;
and over his/her head and all around him/her, Shechinah,
may he/she rest within your wings.

לֶךְ\לְכִי לְשָׁלוֹם.

Leich/l'chi l'shalom.

Go in peace.

Final Confessional Prayer

I acknowledge before the Source of all that life and death
   are not in my hands.
May it come to pass that I may be healed, but if death is my
   fate, then I accept it with dignity
and the loving calm of one who knows the way of all things.

May my death be honorable, and may my life be a healing
   memory for those who know me.
May my loved ones think well of me and may my memory
   bring them joy.

From all those I may have hurt, I ask forgiveness.
Upon all who have hurt me, I bestow forgiveness.

As a wave returns to the ocean, so I return to the Source
   from which I came.

שְׁמַע יִשְׂרָאֵל, יְהֹוָה אֱלֹהֵינוּ, יְהֹוָה אֶחָד.

Sh'ma Yisrael, Adonai Eloheinu, Adonai Echad.

Hear, O Israel, that which we call God is Oneness itself.

Blessed is the Way of God
the Way of Life and Death,
of coming and going,
of meeting and loving,
now and forever.
As I was blessed with the one,
so now am I blessed with the other.
Shalom. Shalom. Shalom.

Vidui

I acknowledge before You, my God and God of my people,
    that my life and my death are in Your hand.
The soul You placed within me is pure: You breathed it
    into me.
You have guarded it all these days;
You take it from me, You will restore it in time to come. In
    Your hand are the souls of all who live and die and the
    breath of every being. Into Your hand I release my spirit.
I am thankful before You, my God; I have treasured my days.
Sustained by times I lived well, touching others with good-
    ness and beauty. I am glad for choices that lifted me
    up, and for the opportunity to be a spark of light to the
    world.
I am grateful for the help and kindness that have always
    accompanied me.
I regret the times I did not choose well:
    times I was too hurt or frightened to see my way,
    times I was too confused or angry to follow my best
    intentions.
My heart aches for words I could not say and for those
    better left unspoken;
for actions I could not take and for those I might rather not
    have taken.
Comfort me with forgiveness, Adonai.
Let me be remembered for the good.

In Your endless compassion, sustain my loved ones.

Bring comfort to them and all who mourn, and let their spirits be renewed in the fullness of Your love.

My God, please sustain my family. In Your endless compassion please bless each one and protect them. Bring comfort to my loved ones and to all who mourn, and let their spirits be renewed in the fullness of Your love.

My God, gather me to my people and grant me my portion in *Gan Eden*.

שְׁמַע יִשְׂרָאֵל, יְהֹוָה אֱלֹהֵינוּ, יְהֹוָה אֶחָד.

Sh'ma Yisrael, Adonai Eloheinu, Adonai echad.

Hear O Israel, Adonai is our God, Adonai is One.

Ending Life Support /
Making an End-of-Life Decision

Adonai, please help us as we face this terrible decision. Bring us close to You so that we feel less alone. Holding on and letting go are two impossible opposites, and yet here we stand, at the bedside of the one we love so much, trying to do both.

Please, God, take gently, enfold him/her under your protective wings and care for him/her always, even as we tried to do in life. Give us strength as we prepare to meet the world without him/her, and guide us as we face the days ahead.

שְׁמַע יִשְׂרָאֵל, יְהוָה אֱלֹהֵינוּ, יְהוָה אֶחָד.
בָּרוּךְ שֵׁם כְּבוֹד מַלְכוּתוֹ לְעוֹלָם וָעֶד.

Sh'ma Yisrael, Adonai Eloheinu, Adonai Echad.
Baruch shem k'vod malchuto l'olam va-ed.

Hear, O Israel, Adonai is our God, Adonai is One.
Blessed is God's glorious majesty forever and ever.

Part III
Living in a Tent of Healing

*Among the miracles of the modern era is that we are able
to live with illness in ways that were once only a prayerful
hope. From addiction to any other condition that is continu-
ally responsive to the most current medical interventions, we
continue to live with the support of many different kinds of
caregivers. When we live in a Tent of Healing it is important
to stay in contact with those around us who can sustain us
in the midst of the inevitable challenges of living with an ongoing illness or condition. For example, an alcoholic who must
take pain medication also needs to maintain a close relationship with his/her recovery community, just as one might stay
informed of every experimental drug protocol that might
sustain one's body in the midst of an active cancer. We hope
that this section offers the sustenance that is necessary when
one enters into a lifestyle that must constantly adjust to the
limitations illness can bring.*

Many Are My Heart's Distresses

Many are my heart's distresses;
let me know Your ways,
Eternal One;
teach me Your paths. (Psalm 25:17, 25:4)

May I not think merely of what I cannot do,
being sick or weak,
but of what I can do,
in spite of weakness and sickness.
Everyone can do something.

Mi Shebeirach for Chronic Illness

Eternal God, I ask for mercy and compassion for myself, burdened with chronic illness. Compassionate One, give me the strength and courage to face the daily challenges in my life. Give me and my loved ones hope for the future and at the same time, acceptance of the present. Help me to find a path toward spiritual wholeness. Be by my side. Help me to know that You are with me at all times, even in times of doubt. Source of Healing, comfort me and bring healing to my soul. Amen.

Upon Receiving a Diagnosis of Dementia

God of compassion, in this moment of fear and dread I turn to You. Lead me through the wilderness; speak to me with tenderness—for You are my hope.

Here, in a foreign land of illness, I long for the familiar: the gentle comfort of loved ones, places I know, things I enjoy. May these sustain me and keep me connected to the world. Bless my days with tiny joys.

And let there be unhurried time with family and friends. I pray that, when I am weak, their arms will embrace me. I pray that, in my silences, they will understand me. In valleys of darkness, may their voices guide me and reassure me. I give thanks for the gift of their patience and love.

May solace come in the sweetness of song, in the beauty of nature, in feelings too deep for words. God, be with me when I feel alone. Accompany my loved ones as they walk in the shadow of my illness.

When confusion takes hold, soothe my spirit; calm my fears. My God of compassion, answer me. And even when I cannot ask, answer me. Heal and comfort those who are ill. Lead us through the wilderness—for You are our hope.

Facing Dementia

My God, I am about to enter a wilderness.
All that I have thought is me—
my voice, my thinking, my memories—
will slip away, and I may not even comprehend it.

As I enter this wilderness my step quivers and my
　　soul hurts.
In this leap of faith I will come to rely on so many,
　　and we will all rely on You.

Whom will I recognize? Who will recognize me?
Even though my mind will change, please do not let
　　the knitting of my soul unravel.
Only You will know me, even if I do not know myself.

Please help me to remember that others before me
　　have found You in the wilderness.
I am not sure I will know to look for You.
But please, look for me.

Entering a Long-Term Care Facility

Comforting God, You are known by many names. Help me to remember that one is *HaMakom*, The Place. Although I no longer live in the place I used to call home, help me to know that You are here with me in this place. Guide and sustain me as I adjust to new rhythms, new people, new dependence, and new losses. Help me to find the place in my heart to build new, meaningful connections here as I learn to call this new place home. Reassure me that I can find laughter, kindness, friendship, and purpose here in this place, just as I did in the home I left. May this be Your will, *HaMakom*. Amen.

Saying Good-bye after a Visit

God of compassion,

As You witness our lives, You know that we travel some roads together and some alone. Sometimes we are like Naomi and Ruth, walking together. At other times, we are like Orpah, kissing Naomi farewell and walking alone.

God of Companionship, comfort us all as we say farewell at the end of this visit. Soothe us as we experience the complicated emotions that accompany this good-bye. Hold us in Your divine love so that we can hold each other in our imperfect human compassion. Remind us that You are present in all journeys—those taken together and those taken alone.

Amen.

Blessing before Eating
for Those Struggling with an Eating Disorder

Source of the soul's nourishment, I find myself struggling, perhaps unable in this moment, to offer gratitude for physical nourishment. Just as our desert ancestors resisted Your manna, I feel the impulse to resist this food. As I tread through my wilderness of confusion and anger, I ask You to guide me onto a path toward well-being, that I may find the strength to affirm life. Though I wrestle with gratitude, I pray for Your help in opening my mouth and my soul to accepting Your nourishment.

אֲדֹנָי, שְׂפָתַי תִּפְתָּח, וּפִי יַגִּיד תְּהִלָּתֶךָ.

Adonai, s'fatai tiftach, ufi yagid t'hilatecha.
Adonai, open up my lips, that my mouth may utter
Your praise.

Addiction

I am in the depth of behavior so repetitive
   that I have lost my breath and cannot think.
I am addicted.
One moment I am confident and the next I am frightened.
In the same instant I feel powerful and weak.
I am pulled between the best and worst of myself.
It is as if I am in a centrifuge spinning so fast
   that I cannot know anything.
God, stop me.
Breathe new life into my lungs.
Give my heart an easier beat.
Calm my soul.
Help me to trust others who know more than I do.
Help me to take one step toward You and the best of who I am.
Please, save me.

Entering Rehab

מִן־הַמֵּצַר קָרָאתִי יָהּ

Min hameitzar karati Yah.

From my narrow place, I am calling out to You, O God.

God, I find myself in this narrow place, where only one thing brings me a fleeting sense of comfort, only one thing brings me joy. I have become a shadow of my former self, forsaking friends, family, and all that I love in my quest for quick and easy gratification.

I know that this is not the true me, that I have gifts to give to others, that I am surrounded by people who love and care for me. You alone, O God, see all and know all, and You know that I am more than this substance that holds me in its grasp. I recall the image of the burning bush in which You appeared to Moses, a bush that burned yet was not consumed. Let me not be consumed; let my true self come through and shine once more. Grant my caregivers the wisdom and compassion to guide me out of this pit to a renewed life. Give me the courage to face the difficult road to recovery. Help me out of the narrowness, O God, that I may return to my full potential.

בָּרוּךְ אַתָּה, יְיָ, מַתִּיר אֲסוּרִים וְזוֹקֵף כְּפוּפִים.

Baruch atah, Adonai, matir asurim v'zokeif k'fufim.

Blessed are You, Adonai, who frees the captive and lifts up the fallen.

When Medicine May Challenge Sobriety

Rofei chol basar / Healer of all flesh: I come before You in
fear and hope:

My physician advises that I take certain medications,
gifts from the world of science that hold out a promise
of relief and healing.

And yet, my struggle with addiction/alcoholism and my
sobriety and recovery lead me to serious reservations and
grave concerns.

In pain, I am vulnerable to old ways of thinking and
patterns of behavior;

I know I am susceptible to fear, self-deception, denial,
and anger.

Help me, Healing One:

> ► To choose a path in open and honest consultation with
> knowledgeable physician(s), my sponsor, therapist,
> and spiritual guides.
>
> May I resist the urge to "know better" than the doctor.
> May I never medicate myself independent of these
> experts.

> ► To be honest regarding the level or kind of pain that I
> can tolerate without medication:
>
> May I not err on the side of taking either too much or
> too little medication.
> May I strictly follow the limits of prescribed dosage
> and timing.

May I consider turning over my prescription to
    another to safeguard my own recovery.

May I continue to discover prayer, meditation, sharing,
    and my recovery literature to transcend discomfort
    and bolster my spirits.

► To reach out and share in order to keep my priorities in
    order and maintain recovery:

seeking out others in recovery who have successfully
    taken medication as prescribed,

gleaning from the experience and insights of members
    who have faced similar situations;

avoiding loneliness, despair, and self-pity by drawing
    on the stories, strength, and hope of meetings.

Highest Power: You know the disease of addiction is cunning, baffling, and powerful and that honesty is the solution:

Guide me to maintain recovery as I reach for health and healing. Amen.

Before Incarceration

My God, I am not quite sure how I got here. I am frightened and confused. I must trust many people, I am not sure how. Suddenly I am in a strange place. It has its own rules. I am not sure how to even act. I need help. Be with me as I walk this difficult path. Please give me succor in this barren place. As I deepen my relationship with You, help me to speak wisely, to see clearly, and to walk Your paths. Amen.

For One Imprisoned

Holy One who blessed our ancestors: I am in a place that challenges my being, my dignity, and my faith. Many among me are unaware of Jewish tradition. Some seem to harbor prejudice that pains my soul. I must be open to You and my tradition in ways I may not have been in the past. I am like those Children of Israel who lived under a ruler who did not know them. I know I cannot leave this place and have discovered that the rhythms of Jewish life nourish me here in ways that I never considered in an open society. I pray that as I consider the constancy of our religious rhythms in daily prayer, dietary mitzvot, and holiday observance, dressing myself in *kippah* and prayer shawl, I will be reminded to seek You. I am grateful, O Holy One, for each and every moment when I am aware of my connection to You, my community, and my faith. I echo Your servant Maimonides in his hope that in a place of *mitzrayim*, narrowness, I be released from any duress put upon my free exercise of these sacred acts. I pray that any embarrassment I carry is not a blockage to all I can do to improve relationships with those around me. Please guide me through the path of reconciliation with those I love. I ask You to grant me my portion of *shalom* and *sh'leimut*, peace and wholeness, so that I can take my place in our community's relationship to You. Amen.

A Prayer of Healing for Mental Illness

May the One who blessed our ancestors bless me with strength and healing as I struggle with emotional distress and mental suffering. May I walk in the footsteps of Jacob, King Saul, Miriam, Hannah, and Naomi, who lived with dark moods, hopelessness, isolation, and terror, but survived and led our people. Just as our father Jacob spent the night wrestling with an angel and prevailed, may I be granted the endurance to wrestle with pain and prevail, night upon night. Grant me the faith to know that though, like Jacob, I may be wounded, shaped, and renamed by this struggle, still I will live on to continue an ever-unfolding, unpredictable path toward healing. May I not be alone on this path but accompanied by family in all its forms, friends, caregivers, ancestors, and the Divine Presence. Surround me with loving-kindness, grace, and companionship, and spread over me a *sukkat shalom*, a shelter of peace and wholeness.

TRAUMA

Seeking Comfort in Distress

God, I seek comfort in my distress. Give me the wisdom
to know that You are with me even now. I am shaken and
uncertain—help me to remember that I have within myself
the power to be healed. I feel isolated and cut off—help me
to remember that I am not alone. Help me to overcome my
pain, my anger, and my fear and to accept the help of those
who care for me. Give me strength to return the love of family, friends, and community. Show me the path of life so that
I can return with a whole heart.

Afterword

Any encounter with the world of medicine naturally stimulates spiritual reflection. Whether concerning the universal human experiences of illness and approaching the end of life, or the specific experiences of pregnancy, child rearing, or pain management, our souls yearn for succor. All spiritual reflection reasonably yearns for communal support.

Prayer by its very nature is filled with metaphor and relationship. Our hope is that the words on these pages have offered a constellation of comfort—some clarity, some insight, some affirmation—and that this solace has guided the spiritual journey toward wholeness.

While this book was not written to be read from cover to cover as one would other literature, it does represent the eternal desire to form a narrative that simultaneously speaks to each of us as uniquely created in God's image and as a part of our greater communal conversation.

Whether you have used this book for inspiration at a glance or in a moment of deep need, we hope that when you close its covers, it has left you with a richer cultivation of your spiritual life, more deeply stimulated to God, Torah, and Israel, and with a broader capacity for resilience.

Additional Resources

These resources are intended to provide further inspiration but are not meant to be exhaustive. We encourage you to explore the resources that will be of help to you.

FOR FURTHER READING

Address, Richard. *Caring for the Soul: R'fuat HaNefesh; A Mental Health Resource and Study Guide.* New York: URJ Press, 2003.

Address, Richard. *Seekers of Meaning.* New York: URJ Press, 2011.

Address, Richard. *To Honor and Respect: A Program and Resource Guide for Congregations on Sacred Aging.* New York: URJ Press, 2005.

Address, Richard, and the Department of Jewish Family Concerns, eds. *A Time to Prepare.* New York: UAHC Press, 2002.

Address, Richard, and Hara Person, eds. *That You May Live Long: Caring for Our Aging Parents, Caring for Ourselves.* New York: URJ Press, 2003.

Cutter, William, ed. *Healing and the Jewish Imagination: Spiritual and Practical Perspectives on Judaism and Health.* Woodstock, VT: Jewish Lights, 2007.

Cutter, William. *Midrash and Medicine: Healing Body and Soul in the Jewish Interpretive Tradition.* Woodstock, VT: Jewish Lights, 2010.

Freeman, David, and Judith Abrams. *Illness and Health in the Jewish Tradition: Writings from the Bible to Today.* Philadelphia: Jewish Publication Society, 1999.

Goldstein, Rafael. *Being A Blessing: 54 Ways You Can Help People Living with Illness.* Dynamicsofhope.com, 2009.

Haberman, Joshua O. *Healing Psalms: Dialogues with God That Help You Cope with Life.* Hoboken, NJ: Wiley, 2003.

Kushner, Harold. *The Lord Is My Shepherd: Healing Wisdom of the Twenty-Third Psalm.* New York: Random House, 2003.

Kushner, Harold. *When Bad Things Happen to Good People*. New York: Schocken Books, 1981.

Levy, Naomi. *Hope Will Find You: My Search for the Wisdom to Stop Waiting and Start Living*. New York: Harmony Books, 2010.

Levy, Naomi. *Talking to God: Personal Prayers for Times of Joy, Sadness, Struggle, and Celebration*. New York: Knopf, 2002.

Levy, Naomi. *To Begin Again: The Journey toward Comfort, Strength, and Faith in Difficult Times*. New York: Ballantine, 1999.

Litapayach Tikvah: To Nourish Hope—Eating Disorders: Perceptions and Perspectives in Jewish Life Today. New York: Union of American Hebrew Congregations Department of Jewish Family Concerns / UAHC Youth Division / Women of Reform Judaism, 2001.

Mencher, Edythe Held. *Resilience of the Soul: Developing Emotional and Spiritual Resilience in Adolescents and Their Families*. New York: URJ Press, 2007.

National Center for Jewish Healing. *A Leader's Guide to Services and Prayers of Healing*. New York: National Center for Jewish Healing, 1996.

National Center for Jewish Healing. *The Outstretched Arm* (newsletter of NCJH). Also available: *Mi Shebeirach* card and *Evening and Morning: A Circle of Prayer* (a *bikur cholim* card).

Olitzky, Kerry M. *100 Blessings Every Day: Daily Twelve Step Recovery Affirmations, Exercises for Personal Growth and Renewal Reflecting Seasons of the Jewish Year*. Woodstock, VT: Jewish Lights, 1993.

Olitzky, Kerry M. *Jewish Paths toward Healing and Wholeness: A Personal Guide to Dealing with Suffering*. Woodstock, VT: Jewish Lights, 2000.

Out of the Depths: Personal Stories of Illness and Healing. New York: National Center for Jewish Healing, 1995.

Perlman, Debbie. *Flames to Heaven: New Psalms for Healing and Praise*. Wilmette, IL: Rad Publishers, 1998.

Person, Hara, ed. *The Mitzvah of Healing: An Anthology of Jewish Texts, Meditations, Essays, Personal Stories, and Rituals*. New York: URJ Press, 2003.

Sonsino, Rifat, and Daniel B. Syme. *Finding God: Selected Responses*. New York: URJ Press, 2002.

Spitz, Elie Kaplan, and Erica Shapiro Taylor. *Healing from Despair: Choosing Wholeness in a Broken World*. Woodstock, VT: Jewish Lights, 2008.

Teutsch, David, ed. *Behoref Ha-yamim: In the Winter of Life*. Wyncote, PA: RRC Press, 2002.

Washofsky, Mark. *Jewish Living: A Guide to Contemporary Reform Practice*. Rev. ed. New York: URJ Press, 2010.

Weintraub, Simkha Y., ed. *Healing of Soul, Healing of Body*. Woodstock, VT: Jewish Lights, 1994.

Weintraub, Simkha Y., with Aaron M. Lever. *Guide Me Along the Way: A Spiritual Companion for Surgery*. New York: National Center for Jewish Healing, 2001.

ORGANIZATIONS

American Pregnancy Association
(972) 550-0140
E-mail: questions@AmericanPregnancy.org

Al-Anon Family Groups
www.al-anon.alateen.org
Family Groups Headquarters: (757) 563-1600
E-mail: wso@al-anon.org

Alcoholics Anonymous
www.aa.org
A.A. World Services: (212) 870-3400
E-mail: tf@aa.org

Canadian Alliance on Mental Illness: camimh.ca

Canadian Mental Health Association: cmha.ca

JACS (Jewish Alcoholics, Chemically Dependent Persons,
and Significant Others)
www.jbfcs.org/JACS
(212) 632-4600

Hospice Foundation of America
www.hospicefoundation.org
(202) 457-5811 or (800) 854-3402
E-mail: hfaoffice@hospicefoundation.org

National Fertility Support Center
www.fertilitysupportcenter.org
(616) 455-1499
E-mail: info@fertilitysupportcenter.org

National Hospice and Palliative Care Organization
www.nhpco.org
Helpline: (800) 658-8898
E-mail: nhpco_info@nhpco.org

The National Infertility Association
www.resolve.org
(703) 556-7172
E-mail: info@resolve.org

HEALING CENTERS

Bay Area Jewish Healing Center
www.jewishhealingcenter.org
(415) 750-4197
E-mail: jewishhealing@ioaging.org

Kalsman Institute on Judaism and Health
Hebrew Union College-Jewish Institute of Religion
huc.edu/kalsman
(213) 749-3424
E-mail: kalsman@huc.edu

The National Center for Jewish Healing
www.jbfcs.org/NCJH
(212) 582-9100
E-mail: admin@jbfcs.org
(Contains state-by-state directory of local healing centers)

ORGANIZATIONS OUTSIDE NORTH AMERICA

AUSTRALIA
AA in Australia: aa.org.au
Australian Institute of Health and Welfare: aihw.gov.au
Mental Illness Fellowship of Australia: mifa.org.au

CANADA
AA in Canada: aacanada.com

ISRAEL
AA in Israel: aa-Israel.org
The Israeli Association for Mental Health: enosh.org.il

Life's Door: lifesdoor.org

NEW ZEALAND
AA in New Zealand: aa.org.nz
Mental Health Foundation of New Zealand: mentalhealth.org.nz
Supporting Families in Mental Illness New Zealand:
supportingfamiliesnz.org.nz

UNITED KINGDOM
AA in The United Kingdom: alcoholics-anonymous.org.uk
United Kingdom: Dept. of Health: dh.gov.uk
United Kingdom: National Health Service: nhs.uk

Sources

2   Traditional *Mi Shebeirach* (male), in *Rabbi's Manual* © 1988 by the Central Conference of American Rabbis, p. 195.

3   Traditional *Mi Shebeirach* (female), in *Rabbi's Manual* © 1988 by the Central Conference of American Rabbis.

4   *Mi Shebeirach* © Debbie Friedman. Used by permission of the Estate of Debbie Friedman.

5   *Mi Shebeirach*, by Rabbi Thomas M. Alpert. Reprinted by permission.

6   Prayer for Comfort and Healing, by Rabbi Eric Weiss. Reprinted by permission.

7   Meditation on Healing, by Rabbi Naomi Levy, in *To Begin Again: The Journey toward Comfort, Strength and Hope in Difficult Times* © 1998 by Ballantine Books/ Random House. Reprinted by permission of International Creative Management, Inc. Copyright © 1998 by Naomi Levy.

8   Prayer for God's Love © Rabbi Rami Shapiro. Reprinted by permission.

9   Psalm Eighty-Five, by Debbie Perlman in *Flames to Heaven: New Psalms for Healing and Praise* © 1998 by Debbie Perlman, Rad Publishers, Wilmette, Ill., p. 115. Reprinted by permission of Dr. Reid Perlman.

12   Prayer for Mercy, in *Gates of Healing: A Message of Comfort and Hope* by the Central Conference of American Rabbis, p. 5.

13   Needing Help, source unknown.

14 The Plague of Darkness, by Debbie Perlman. Reprinted by permission of Dr. Reid Perlman.

15 Take My Hand, by Rabbi Eric Weiss. Reprinted by permission.

16 Surround Me with Stillness, by Debbie Perlman. Reprinted by permission of Dr. Reid Perlman.

17 Psalm One Hundred Ninety-Nine, by Debbie Perlman. Used by permission of Dr. Reid Perlman.

18 When Fears Multiply, by Rabbi Hershel Matt, appeared as "*Hashkiveinu*" in *Raayanot* 3, no. 2 (Spring 1983) © by the Reconstructionist Rabbinical Association. Reprinted by permission.

19 Parents' *Mi Shebeirach for a Child*, by Rabbi Hara Person.

20 A Child's *Mi Shebeirach*, by Rabbi Eric Weiss.

21 A Prayer for Those Who Help, by Susan Feldman. Adapted from the liturgy: Service of Healing created at Congregation Sha'ar Zahav of San Francisco, 1988. Reprinted by permission.

22 A Medical Practitioner's Prayer, by Rabbi Eric Weiss. Reprinted by permission.

24 On Being Unable to Participate in Jewish Life, by Rabbi Jon Sommer.

25 On Being Distant, by Rabbi Jon Sommer.

26 On Anxiety, by Rabbi Chaim Stern, in *On the Doorposts of Your House*, Revised Edition © 1994, 2010 by the Central Conference of American Rabbis, p. 163.

27 New Chances, by Rabbi Pearl Barlev, from "Fear to Comfort." Reprinted by permission.

28 Today Has Been So Hard, by Rabbi Simkha Weintraub, LCSW, in "Caretaking," *The Outstretched Arm* (NCJH) 4, no. 1 (Winter 2002) © 2002–3 by JBFCS/JACS and National Center for Jewish Healing. Reprinted by permission.

29 Prayer for Surgery, by Rabbi Perry Rank.

30 A Prayer for One Approaching Surgery or Crisis, in *Gates of Healing: A Message of Comfort and Hope* © by the Central Conference of American Rabbis, p. 15.

31 A Child's Surgery, © 2012 by Alden Solovy and www.tobendlight. com. Reprinted by permission.

32 *Asher Yatzar* (The One Who Forms), by Rabbi Elliot Kukla.

33 For Beginning Treatment, by Rabbi Alan Cook. Reprinted with permission.

34 For Ongoing Treatment, by Rabbi Hara Person and Rabbi Eric Weiss.

36 Prayer before Chemotherapy, by Rabbi Nina Beth Cardin.

37 Upon Conclusion of Treatment, by Rabbi Alan Cook. Reprinted with permission.

38 Choosing to End Treatment, by Rabbi Alan Cook. Reprinted with permission.

39 Hopeless, by Shoshana Hadassah. Reprinted with permission.

40 Abortion, by Rabbi Hara E. Person.

41 *Birkat Hagomeil* (For One Who Has Escaped Peril), by Rabbi Jack Bloom © 2006. Reprinted by permission.

42 On Coming Out of Dark Places, by Kevin Johnson, in *Siddur Sha'ar Zahav* © 2009 by Congregation Sha'ar Zahav, p. 41.

43 Like a Wave Arising, by Rabbi Rami Shapiro. Reprinted by permission.

44 On Recovery, by Rabbi Chaim Stern, in *On the Doorposts of Your House*, Revised Edition © 1994, 2010 by the Central Conference of American Rabbis, p. 163.

45 Prayer for Transitioning Gender, by Rabbi Elliot Kukla. Reprinted by permission.

46 A Prayer during a Difficult Pregnancy, by Rabbi Noami Levy, in *Talking to God: Personal Prayers for Times of Joy, Sadness, Struggle and Celebration* © 2002 by Doubleday / Random House, p. 74. Reprinted by permission of International Creative Management, Inc. Copyright © 2002 by Naomi Levy.

47 Celebrating a Healthy Birth, adapted by Rabbi Chaim Stern from a prayer by Rabbi Sandy Eisenberg Sasso, in an unpublished manuscript edited by Rabbi Barton Lee for *Rabbi's Manual*, vol.

2. It appears in *On the Doorposts of Your House*, Revised Edition © 1994, 2010 by Central Conference of American Rabbis, p. 127.

48 Blessing for a Premature Birth, by Rabbi Elliot Kukla. Reprinted by permission.

49 Things That Are Not to Be, by Rabbi Hanna Yerushalami. Reprinted by permission.

51 On Miscarriage or Stillbirth, by Anonymous. In *Siddur Sha'ar Zahav* © 2009 by Congregation Sha'ar Zahav. Reprinted by permission.

52 A Prayer When One Experiences Infertility, by Rabbi Naomi Levy, in *Talking to God: Personal Prayers for Times of Joy, Sadness, Struggle and Celebration* © 2002 by Doubleday / Random House. Reprinted by permission of International Creative Management, Inc. Copyright © 2002 by Naomi Levy.

53 A Prayer for Accepting Infertility and Exploring Adoption, by Rabbi Naomi Levy, in *Talking to God: Personal Prayers for Times of Joy, Sadness, Struggle and Celebration* © 2002 by Doubleday / Random House, p. 89. Reprinted by permission of International Creative Management, Inc. Copyright © 2002 by Naomi Levy.

54 Accepting Infertility, by Rabbi Hara E. Person.

55 Accepting Infertility: For a Man, by Rabbi Eric Weiss.

56 Before a Transplant, by Rabbi Eric Weiss. Reprinted by permission.

57 After a Transplant, by Rabbi Hara E. Person.

58 Prayer for Going Home, by Rabbi Shira Stern. Reprinted by permission.

60 *T'filat HaDerech*, © Debbie Friedman. Used by the permission of the Estate of Debbie Friedman.

60 *Shehecheyanu*. Translation from *Mishkan T'filah: A Reform Siddur*, edited by Rabbi Elyse Frishman, © 2007 by the Central Conference of American Rabbis. Translation by Rabbi Eric Weiss.

61 Prayer for Renewing Connections with God, by Debbie Perlman. Used by permission of Dr. Reid Perlman.

91 A Prayer of Healing for Mental Illness, by Rabbi Elliot Kukla.
    Reprinted by permission.

92 Seeking Comfort in Distress, by Rabbi Chaim Stern, in *On the
    Doorposts of Your House*, Revised Edition © 1994, 2010 by the
    Central Conference of American Rabbis, pp. 164–65.

The Editor

Rabbi Eric Weiss *is CEO/president of the Bay Area Jewish Healing Center (BAJHC). Alongside the National Center for Jewish Healing, BAJHC was the first Jewish Healing Center in the country. BAJHC provides Jewish spiritual care to those who are ill, dying, and bereaved (www.jewishhealingcenter.org). Rabbi Weiss was ordained at the New York campus of Hebrew Union College–Jewish Institute of Religion in 1989. He is formally trained in Jewish education, clinical chaplaincy, and spiritual direction. He is a spiritual direction supervisor, and he has served on the CCAR national board and as a national CCAR rabbinic mentor. He holds a BA with honors from the University of California, Santa Cruz. He is a co-founder of "Grief and Growing:™ A Healing Weekend for Individuals and Families in Mourning" and "Kol Haneshama: Jewish Hospice/End of Life Care Volunteer Program." He lives with his husband, Dan, in San Francisco, California.*